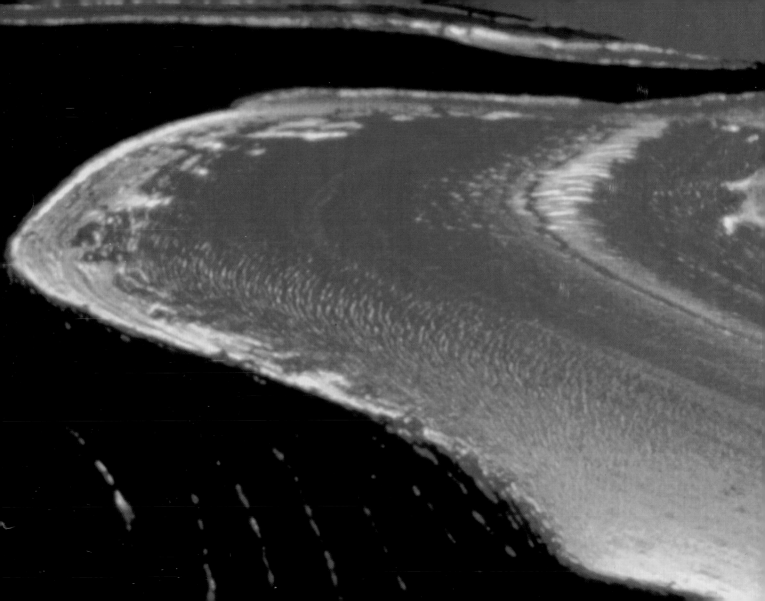

VOLCANO!

An **EXPLOSIVE** Tour of Earth's Hot Spots

by Bill Haduch

Dutton Children's Books • New York

FOR NITA, THE LAVA OF MY LIFE

Special thanks to Dr. R. V. Fisher, a great volcanologist, a great writer, and an all-around great guy

Discovery Communications, Inc.
John S. Hendricks, Founder, Chairman, and Chief Executive Officer
Judith A. McHale, President and Chief Operating Officer
Clark Bunting II, Executive Vice President and General Manager, *Animal Planet*
Judy L. Harris, Senior Vice President, Consumer and Educational Products

Discovery Publishing
Stephen Newstedt, Vice President
Rita Mullin, Editorial Director
Michael Hentges, Design Director
Mary Kalamaras, Senior Editor
Rick Ludwick, Managing Editor

Discovery Kids™, which includes Saturday and Sunday morning programming on Discovery Channel®, Discoverykids.com, and the digital showcase network, is dedicated to encouraging and empowering kids to explore the world around them.

Discovery Kids™ is a trademark of Discovery Communications, Inc.

Published in the United States 2001 by Dutton Children's Books,
a division of Penguin Putnam Books for Young Readers
345 Hudson Street, New York, New York 10014
www.penguinputnam.com

Designed by Dan Hosek
Edited by Meredith Mundy Wasinger

Printed in China
First Edition
2 4 6 8 10 9 7 5 3 1
ISBN 0-525-46479-4 (paperback)
ISBN 0-525-46775-0 (hardcover)

Photo Credits
p. 4: (bottom) © Roger Ressmeyer/CORBIS.
p. 5: (bottom) © Jim Sugar Photography/CORBIS.
p. 6: © Jim Sugar Photography/CORBIS.
p. 7: (center) © Daniel Lainé/CORBIS; (bottom) © COREL.
p. 8: © Douglas Peebles/CORBIS.
p. 9: Mehau Kulyk/Science Photo Library.
p. 12: © Roger Ressmeyer/CORBIS.
p. 13: (top) © Roger Ressmeyer/CORBIS; (bottom) © Genevieve Leaper; Ecoscene/CORBIS.
p. 14: (top left) © Ralph White/CORBIS; (top right) © Roger Ressmeyer/CORBIS; (bottom) © Ted Streshinsky/CORBIS.
p. 15: (top) © Paul A. Souders/CORBIS.
p. 16: (top) © Jim Sugar/CORBIS.
p. 17: (center) © Michael S. Yamashita/CORBIS.
p. 18: (bottom) © Adam Woolfitt/CORBIS.
p. 19: (top) © Roger Ressmeyer/CORBIS; (center) © Danny Lehman/CORBIS.
p. 20: (top and center right) © Roger Ressmeyer/CORBIS; (bottom left) © Jonathan Blair/CORBIS; (bottom right) © Vittoriano Rastelli/CORBIS.
p. 21: (top) © David Muench/CORBIS; (bottom) © Sergio Dorantes/CORBIS.
p. 22: (top) © Mark Gibson/CORBIS; (bottom) © Roger Ressmeyer/CORBIS.
p. 23: (top left: gold bar) © CORBIS; (top right: diamonds) © Dave G. Houser/CORBIS; (center: gold coins) © Adam Woolfitt/CORBIS.
p. 24: (bottom left and right) © Roger Ressmeyer/CORBIS.
p. 25: (bottom left) © Michael S. Yamashita/CORBIS; (bottom right) © Wolfgang Kaehler/CORBIS.
p. 26: © Roger Ressmeyer/CORBIS.
p. 27: (top and center) Maurice and Katia Krafft, Krafft/Explorer/Science Source/Photo Researchers, Inc.; (bottom) © Michael S. Yamashita/CORBIS.
p. 28: photos courtesy of R.V. Fisher.
p. 29: (bottom) © NASA/Roger Ressmeyer/CORBIS.
p. 31: (center left) © Roger Ressmeyer/CORBIS.

A MONSTER IN THE CORNFIELD

THE EARTH HAD BEEN SHAKING FOR MONTHS. To a farm boy living near the tiny Mexican village of Parícutin (par-EE-koo-teen), little earthquakes were nothing new. It was just that in all his twelve years, Simón Jiménez had never felt so many.

All the quaking gave Simón's neighbors the jitters. But life had to go on. None of the villagers had a car or truck. What could they do? Walk two hundred miles to Mexico City? So they went about their business, planting corn as the Earth trembled beneath their feet.

One February morning in 1943 was different. Everything was still. Simón noticed that even the birds were quiet. No one felt like working or eating, and kids seemed to cling to their parents. Suddenly, the stillness was smashed by a big earthquake, and everyone ran outside. When the shaking stopped, a weird clunking, bubbling noise came from under the ground. Simón thought it sounded like boiling rocks or a giant trying to clear his throat. And then there was the biggest quake of all. Cracks zigzagged across the fields, and Simón imagined the rocks beneath him breaking apart and sliding into a bottomless pit.

In the distance, Simón could see a monstrous cloud of black smoke. Houses must be burning, he thought. When hot black cinders started to fall from the sky, Simón and his parents began to run. Neighbors ran with them, and the news spread through the crowd. It wasn't houses burning. Smoke and cinders were roaring from a hole in the cornfields. Parícutin was turning into a volcano.

HOT FACTS

Without Volcanoes, We're Nothing

Scientists believe that volcanoes originally gave the Earth its oceans and atmosphere by blowing water vapor and other gases out across the surface. One hundred percent of the Earth's surface, all minerals, and everything that feeds on minerals (like us!) were once volcanic material.

Throw Away Your Watch

Volcanic eruptions and explosions may seem quick, but the reasons they happen are spread over amazingly long periods of time. To understand volcanoes, think in Earth time, not human time. Some scientists think that for every minute humans have lived on the Earth, the Earth has been here for thirty hours.

Shaking All Over

The movement of hot, gassy material inside the Earth causes volcanic tremors before and during eruptions. Different from other earthquakes, these tremors help scientists predict eruptions.

Setting up equipment to monitor volcanic tremors is not a job for the timid.

Gone in an Instant

Even the biggest volcanic mountains can disappear instantly. Hot, gassy material can push with an explosive force as powerful as ten thousand atomic bombs. Imagine a mountain two miles high and two miles wide suddenly lifting off the Earth's surface, crumbling, and blowing away in the wind. **Boom!** It happens.

It bulged and it bulged. Then it blew. The eruption and landslide of Mount St. Helens left a gaping crater a mile and a half wide.

Officially It's a Hole, Not a Hill

A volcano is a hole in the Earth's crust that lets melted rock and hot gases escape from the Earth's interior.

Let's Get to the Point

Volcanic mountains are made when melted rock and ash flow or fly out of the hole and settle and harden nearby. Over time, layers and layers of this stuff create a mountain— sometimes pointy, sometimes not.

Hot Lunch

Materials coming out of a volcano are extremely hot—usually about 2,000°F. That's four times hotter than the average kitchen oven. At 2,000°F, a hot dog cooks in about one second. Then it bursts into flames.

> **Ruins of a church destroyed by lava from Parícutin.**

What's New?

There's only one volcano that humans have reported popping up brand-new out of the ground—Parícutin in 1943. All other eruptions we know about have come from existing volcanoes.

> **About fifteen to twenty volcanoes are erupting as you read this.**

> **Magma venting from a volcano under the ocean.**

By the Numbers

No one knows the exact number of volcanoes in the world. Most are under the oceans. About fifteen hundred volcanoes on land are considered "potentially active." That means they have erupted and may erupt again. About 550 of these have erupted during human history.

INTO THE CRATERS

CRUST
About 30 miles thick
(3 to 5 miles thick under
the oceans)

**SOLID
INNER CORE**
About 800 miles across. It radiates
heat at 9,000°F.

**MELTED
LIQUID OUTER CORE**
About 1,400 miles thick

**MELTED
TARLIKE LOWER MANTLE**
About 1,800 miles thick

**DENSE
UPPER MANTLE**
From 20 to 200 miles
thick

Baby, It's Hot Inside

The Earth's inside heat comes from an atomic furnace right at the center—an eight-hundred-mile-wide metal ball crammed solid with iron and nickel atoms. As these atoms decay, they give off radioactivity in the form of heat and light, sort of like a star. In fact, the core of the Earth glows white-hot at 9,000°F. Because the core is so densely packed with atoms, it has great mass, and it creates gravity. The hot core pulls all the Earth's other materials toward it. And guess what? They melt! Surrounding the hot core is thirty-four hundred miles of goo, layer upon layer, oozing and stewing in the heat. Some of the goo is melted liquid. Most of it is hot enough to be liquid, but pressure keeps it more solid like tar. All of it is incredibly hot. Thirty miles from the surface, the stuff is still 2,000°F. On the surface, where the goo meets air and ocean, it cools and hardens into a crust. Three to thirty miles thick, the crust is strong enough to support oceans, mountains, skyscrapers, and even circus elephants. And, most of the time, its rocky thickness protects us from all that nasty heat down there.

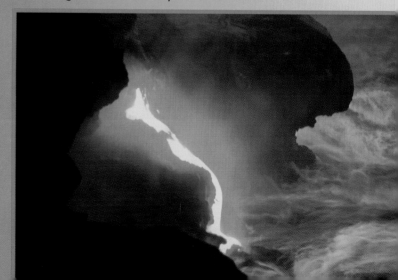

OF VULCAN

If you're on the Earth, you're floating on magma. And if you're reading this in a boat, you're floating twice—on the water above the crust and on the magma below the crust.

The Goo Is Not Called Goo

It's called **schmutz**. Just kidding. Melted material inside the Earth is called magma, and it collects under volcanoes in hollow areas called magma chambers. Just like a simmering stew in a covered kettle, it always wants to find a way out and boil over. When magma does flow out of the Earth's crust, it gets a new name: lava. What's in all this magma and lava? Same stuff you might find in your average backyard rock—silicon, aluminum, iron, oxygen, and everything else that makes up the Earth.

Nice Crust, But It's Cracked

The Earth's crust, on the land and under the sea, is cracked into about a dozen slabs, some big enough to hold entire continents and oceans. The slabs are called tectonic plates, and they float on the hot magma below. In some areas, under the Atlantic Ocean, for example, the plates drift slowly apart from one another. This creates a gap in the crust. Around the edges of the

Plate movement is slow in human time—only about an inch per year. But think in Earth time...In just ten thousand years, each plate would move almost the length of three football fields.

Pacific Ocean, the plates drift toward one another. This causes subduction (sub-DUCK-shun)—one plate's edge slowly works its way under the other plate's edge. The lower plate is forced down into the heat below, and it melts into even more magma. Either way, gaps and subduction along the edges of the plates create just what the magma is looking for—a way out. Most volcanic eruptions take place along tectonic plate boundaries.

North American Plate

Eurasian Plate

Pacific Plate

African Plate

Pacific Plate

Nazca Plate

South American Plate

Indian-Australian Plate

Antarctic Plate

Heard About the Latest Island Hot Spot?

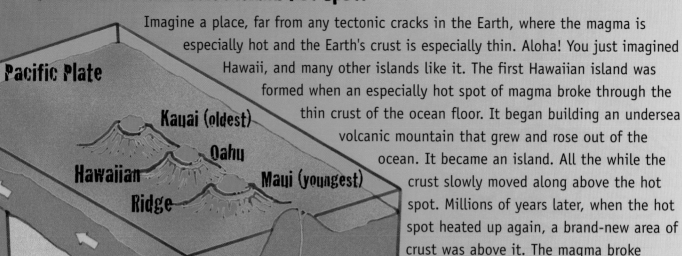

Pacific Plate

Kauai (oldest)

Oahu

Hawaiian Ridge

Maui (youngest)

Solid Dense Rock

Zone of Magma Formation

Imagine a place, far from any tectonic cracks in the Earth, where the magma is especially hot and the Earth's crust is especially thin. Aloha! You just imagined Hawaii, and many other islands like it. The first Hawaiian island was formed when an especially hot spot of magma broke through the thin crust of the ocean floor. It began building an undersea volcanic mountain that grew and rose out of the ocean. It became an island. All the while the crust slowly moved along above the hot spot. Millions of years later, when the hot spot heated up again, a brand-new area of crust was above it. The magma broke through this new area, and over time a whole new island was formed. It happened again and again. Today we have a chain of six major Hawaiian islands, all formed by the same hot spot. And we're not finished. Another undersea volcano is now growing in the moving crust off the coast of Hawaii, fed by the same old hot spot. In a few million years this new volcano may be the seventh Hawaiian island. But it already has a name: Loihi (low-EE-hee). Don't delay! Travel agents are waiting for your call!

Mything the Point

The idea about plates floating around on magma has been well understood only since the 1960s. Before that, many other explanations for volcanoes erupted from the human imagination. A sampling:

The ancient Romans found a smoking island off the coast of Sicily and chose to believe that deep inside, a supernatural blacksmith named Vulcan was busy making lightning. They named the island Vulcano. The island is still there, and so is the English word *volcano*.

Hawaiians blamed eruptions on the goddess Pele, who was thought to dig holes in the Earth with a magic stick. Her home was the crater Halemaumau (hall-eh-MAU-mau), which means "House of Everlasting Fire." Even today, visitors who try to leave Hawaii with lava souvenirs are often warned by locals about Pele's anger.

And the next time you hear people talk about hell, tell them you know where the entrance is—the Mount Hekla volcano in Iceland. At least that's what ancient Icelanders thought.

THE INCREDIBLE ERUPTING EGG

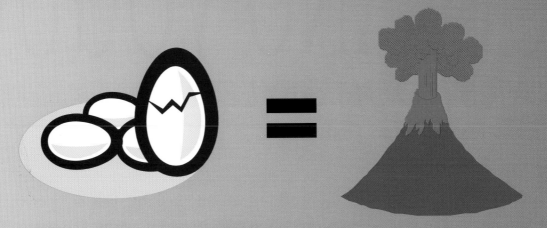

What's the difference between an egg and the Earth? That's easy. An egg is a blob of goo covered by a thin shell. And the Earth? A blob of HOT goo covered by a thin shell. There. Now you know.

What would happen if you made an egg even more like the Earth and gave it crustal plate boundaries? A terrible mess, no doubt. But what if you gave the egg just a little weak spot and heated things up inside? Would you get Hawaii? Let's find out!

1. Bug an adult to get you a small cooking pot and enough water to cover one egg. Put the pot on the stove, but don't turn on the heat yet.

2. Use a pushpin to peck one hole in the rounded (not pointed) end of an uncooked egg. It's probably best to do this over a sink. And don't stick yourself with the pushpin, okay?

3. Poke a wooden toothpick into the pinhole to make the hole a little bigger, about the width of the toothpick. Don't make it so big that the goo just pours out.

4. Put the egg in the cold water, have an adult set the heat to boil the water, and watch. (Not too close!) It'll take a few minutes for the egg's "magma" to heat up and the pressure to build, but when it does... **HAWAII!**

Why This Eggsperiment Is So Eggsiting

1. The eruption is caused by heat like a real volcano (unlike baking soda and vinegar experiments that make it seem like eruptions come from chemical reactions).

2. When you're done, breakfast is ready!

VOLCANO VOGUE

WHAT'S YOUR STYLE?

Today's Hottest Volcano Fashions

by Roxey Rupt, Editor

Devastating beauty best describes the world of volcano fashion. But before you can consider yourself a true volcano fashion hound, you must know the five basic styles:

The Lava Dome

Supermodels fear zits. But even Kate Moss might be fascinated by a volcano that's like a zit ready to pop. It's called the lava dome. Lava domes form when very thick lava forces its way out of the Earth. Too thick to flow, its outer surfaces develop a crust. As more lava gathers inside, the crust cracks and grows, and takes on a domelike shape. A lava dome can actually *be* the volcano, or part of an existing volcano. Pressure building under the crust can eventually blow the dome to smithereens, scattering chunks of crust far and wide. When these babies blow, look out! That's no zit!

The Cinder Cone

The cinder cone volcano usually has the elegant shape of an anthill. A *huge* anthill. Blobs of lava and ashes are blown gracefully into the air. The flying lava hardens and breaks into small jagged rock pieces called cinders. The cinders fall around the hole. *Voilá!* (vwah-LAH—French for "There it is!") You have a cinder cone volcano. It has nothing to do with supermodel "Cinder" Crawford.

Elegance doesn't last forever. Sometimes after an eruption, the empty magma chamber beneath the volcano caves in. The mountain becomes a low spot called a caldera. Some calderas are as large as forty miles across.

The Submarine

Ahoy! Love that nautical look? The Earth is mostly ocean, so that's where most volcanoes are. Also, the Earth's crust is thinner under the oceans, and lava often spews out along undersea tectonic plate boundaries. The weight and coldness of the seawater can do weird things to the hot lava, hardening it into puffy shapes called pillow lava. There are also "smokers"—jets of hot water, gas, and particles. (Smoking is so unfashionable!) Over time, all this material can pile up and rise above the surface of the sea. A stylish new island paradise is born!

Pillow lava created on the ocean floor.

The Shield

They're called shield volcanoes because their flattened shapes once reminded people of warriors' shields. Ooh. The military look. Very chic. Their lava is often thin and runny and flows freely from the main vent in all directions. There are often other vents, too. As layers of runny lava harden, shield volcanoes can become very wide and high, like Hawaii's Mauna Loa, the world's largest active volcano. It rises thirty thousand feet above the ocean floor; almost fourteen thousand feet of it are above sea level. Contrary to Hollywood rumors, actress Brooke Shields did not discover shield volcanoes.

The Composite

Considered the most beautiful and classic volcano style, composite volcanoes, also called stratovolcanoes, are the tall, pointy kind. They're a favorite in Hollywood movies. If you could X-ray a composite volcano, you'd see layer upon layer of ash, cinders, and rock, built over millions of years and many eruptions. You might find a tall central vent full of hardened lava—a "plug." Plus you might find places where lava flowed through cracks in the sides of the volcano and then hardened, creating hard "ribs" on the mountainside. Timeless style. Classic elegance.

Composite volcano style can also fade when erosion wears down its layers. Sometimes only the lava plug is left, like Devil's Tower in Wyoming. Yee-hah! The western look.

FROM BEAUTY TO

IT'S ALWAYS INTERESTING WHEN THINGS EXPLODE.

Party balloons. Firecrackers. Ha-ha. Do it again. But those are little things. What happens when a mountain explodes? Here are some of the beastly things that can happen when a mountain turns itself inside out.

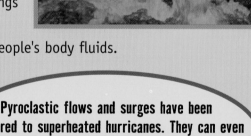

Pyroclastic Flows and Surges

Pyroclastic (PIE-row-class-stick) means "rocks broken by fire." When a volcano erupts, it can send enormous amounts of hot gases, rocks, ash, and lava rocketing skyward. When this stuff crashes to the ground, it can fly down the volcano's slopes at up to two hundred miles per hour in a huge cloud as hot as 1,650°F. The hot, heavy cloud can travel for miles and push over buildings and ships, incinerate plant life, and boil people's body fluids.

Pyroclastic flows and surges have been compared to superheated hurricanes. They can even hit seawater and create a deadly wave called a tsunami (soo-NOM-mee).

Tephra Falls and Ballistic Projectiles

Tephra is anything rocky that falls out of an eruption. It could be cinders, ash, or a fine powder called pumice (PUM-miss). Or it could be bigger rocks, called bombs and blocks. A ballistic projectile is anything rocky that *flies* out of an eruption. Sometimes these rocks are as big as cars and can fly sideways at 250 miles per hour! Ouch! Whether stuff falls or flies, it's rock, and it's heavy. Enough pumice powder landing on a rooftop can crush a house. Like raindrops rushing around in thunder-clouds, tephra particles swirling around above volcanoes often generate dangerous lightning.

BEAST

Lava Flows

A lava flow snaking down a mountainside is the traditional volcano terror. But the truth is that a lava flow rarely kills humans. You can see the lava coming and can usually step out of its way or outrun it. A lava flow will, however, bury, crush, cover, and burn anything that *doesn't* get out of its way. This includes buildings, plant life, and anyone busy watching reruns of *I Lava Lucy*.

Lahars

Question: What happens when a snowy mountain peak is suddenly overcome by tons of superhot eruption debris? Answer: An instant flood called a lahar (luh-HARR). The hot gases, rocks, ash, and lava combine with the melted snow to rush downhill, sweeping away everything they touch. The water can also come from lakes on the volcanic mountain, or even from rainfall.

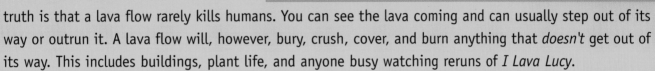

Debris-Flow Avalanches

You've seen the cartoons—sometimes just a shout can cause a snowy avalanche. Well, just imagine what a shuddering volcano can do. Whole rocky wall sections can crumble and roll down the mountainside in a debris-flow avalanche. If you're in its path, well...ever see a cartoon cat get run over by a steamroller?

Volcanic Gas

Heat a rock, and it gives off gases. Superheat a mountain full of rock, and it gives off GASES! Some are good gases like oxygen. Some are deadly like carbon monoxide. Some gases smell terrible. Some have no smell. If the wrong gas flows into the wrong place at the wrong time, humans and animals can suffocate. Volcanic gases can even change weather patterns. And sun shining through the volcanic gases and dust is often the reason for beautiful sunsets.

VOLCANO HALL OF

Mount St. Helens, Washington

The most photographed, most studied volcanic eruption of its time, Mount St. Helens in 1980 helped scientists learn much about how volcanoes work. Throughout the spring, earthquakes and small explosions gave signs that the volcano was waking up after 123 quiet years. Scientists were ready with cameras, measurement equipment, and sampling tools. In spite of all the preparation, the massive eruption killed fifty-seven people, including at least one scientist.

Mount Pelée, Martinique

This volcano is famous for scorching the city of St. Pierre in the Eastern Caribbean in 1902, instantly killing twenty-nine thousand residents and leaving only two survivors. People in St. Pierre felt protected from the volcano's lava by the region's hills and valleys. At the time, no one understood that a pyroclastic flow could bring a 1,650°F glowing cloud of gas and volcanic particles across hills and valleys at two hundred miles per hour. The flow even blasted across the harbor, boiling seawater as it went and flipping over ships like toys.

FLAME

Mount Vesuvius, Italy

Vesuvius is most famous for burying the city of Pompeii (pom-PAY) under twenty-three feet of debris in the year A.D. 79. Almost 1,700 years later, scientists digging at Pompeii began to discover signs of a city stopped dead in its tracks. They found the remains of bread in ovens, paintings, and furniture. But most amazing are the imprints of people and animals pressed into the hardened ash. The ash sometimes even shows facial expressions. Today, the digging goes on. And so does Vesuvius. It erupted several times during the twentieth century, and steam still rises from its crater.

Parícutin, Mexico

In all human history, we know of only one volcano built from scratch. A farmer was plowing his cornfield near the town of Parícutin when the hooves of his oxen began sinking into the ground. Soon steam began to rise from the hoof holes, followed by flying rocks and ash. By the next morning there was a cinder cone thirty feet high in the cornfield. Over the next nine years, the volcano grew to 1,200 feet high and covered the town. And then as suddenly as it started, Parícutin stopped erupting.

Nevado del Ruiz, Colombia

This volcano was topped with a snow-covered glacier until one stormy night in 1985. That's when a so-called tiny eruption scattered lava across the ice. Suddenly, the glacier transformed into a mass of superheated water and rock and raced down the volcano slope, picking up more rock along the way. Now it was a raging, unstoppable lahar. It roared some forty-five miles to sweep away villages in a 120-foot-thick torrent of mud and boulders. The deaths of twenty-three thousand people proved once again that water and volcanoes don't mix.

For more on Hall of Flame members and all kinds of other hot info on volcanoes, visit http://www.discovery.com/exp/ montserrat/topten.html. You can also check out the U.S. Geological Survey website at www.usgs.gov. When you get there, just click on "volcanoes."

VOLCANO HALL OF

Mount Pinatubo, Philippines

Imagine an eruption ten times bigger than that of Mount St. Helens happening near the homes of a million people. That's what happened when Mount Pinatubo erupted in 1991. One of the biggest eruptions of the twentieth century, it shot a massive cloud of ash over nineteen miles into the sky and sent pyroclastic flows and ash into populated areas. Luckily, growing knowledge about volcanoes helped scientists provide good warnings. People had time to evacuate and many lives were saved.

Early Warning Award

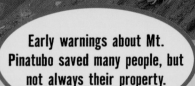

Early warnings about Mt. Pinatubo saved many people, but not always their property.

Mount Etna, Sicily

Old-Timer Award

Europe's largest volcano has been active for over three thousand years! Eruptions were described as early as 1500 B.C., and Etna is mentioned in many ancient writings. It's the most studied volcano on Earth and even one of the most beloved. Frequent eruptions from its four craters produce lava, ash, and spectacular fireworks. But eruptions are so familiar that local residents feel comfortable living on its slopes.

FLAME

Crater Lake, Oregon

The only body of water in the Hall of Flame, Crater Lake was a twelve-thousand-foot composite volcano until seven thousand years ago. Then it erupted and caved into its magma chamber. It became a hole (caldera) two thousand feet deep and six miles wide. Heavy snowfall and rain over many years filled the caldera, but not before a new cinder cone volcano popped out of the bottom and became an island. An ancient eruption, a caldera that became one of the world's deepest and most beautiful lakes, and a cinder cone island make the Crater Lake region a volcanic wonderland.

Mount Tambora, Indonesia

The deadliest volcano in recorded history, it killed over ninety thousand people when it exploded in 1815. Most died from starvation and disease when ash ruined farmland and spoiled water supplies. A year later, dust in the air still blocked enough sunlight to change weather and hurt crops all over the world. Tambora is even blamed for a June 1816 snowfall in New England that marked "The Year Without Summer."

Mount Krakatau, Indonesia

Krakatau has the honor of creating the loudest sound ever experienced by humans. Imagine a noise in Los Angeles being heard in New York—that's about the volume of Krakatau's 1883 explosion. The sound broke stone walls two hundred miles away. Scientists say the explosion was probably caused by seawater leaking into the magma chamber, creating steam pressure, and blowing the cinder cone seventeen miles into the sky. Krakatau's biggest killers were tsunamis, which raced clear across the Pacific Ocean.

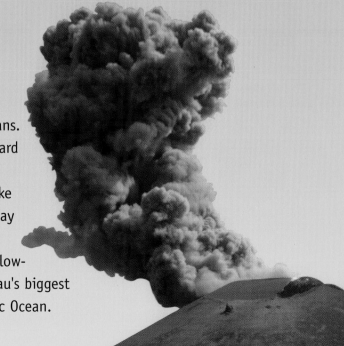

THE LAVA LAMP AND

Lava Las Vegas!

People who say you can't predict when a volcano will erupt have not been to Las Vegas. This famous city in the Nevada desert has a fake Statue of Liberty, a fake Eiffel Tower, and a fake beach with fake waves. Why not a fake volcano? The fifty-four-foot-high concrete cone "erupts" every fifteen minutes, shooting propane gas flames and red-colored water skyward. Meanwhile, loudspeakers rumble so deeply that some people report feeling the ground shake. The crowds love it. Sometimes so many wait for the blasts that people have to stand across the street just to get a good view. Brides and grooms have gotten married in front of the volcano, waiting for just the perfect time during an eruption to say, "I do!" And as if that's not enough, a ghost-watching group reports that the volcano may be haunted. But this is Las Vegas...They're probably just fake ghosts.

Q: What did the teacher volcano do when the student volcanoes would not be quiet? A: He blew his top!

It's a Lamp All Right, but It's Not Lava

The colored blob in those weird lava lamps from the 1960s has nothing to do with volcanoes—it's usually dyed paraffin wax and mineral oil in water.

Volcanic Cleanup

Does your school have a lavatory? Know why it's called a LAVAtory? Because in many languages, *lava* means "to clean." Crushed lava powder, called pumice, can be used to scrub dirt out of many things, even skin. Mechanics often use lava soap on their hands. And pumice is a favorite of professional window washers.

OTHER ODDITIES

You'll Find the Darndest Stuff in a Volcano

Diamonds are created deep in the Earth's crust by heat and pressure and are almost always found in old, eroded volcanic holes called kimberlite pipes. Gold, silver, and all precious metals are also created by volcanic action. Volcanoes can even make some rocks magnetic by baking their electrons into a certain pattern.

Did you hear about the Valentine's Day card that popped out of a volcano's crater? It said, "Do you lava me like I lava you?"

Whose Side Are You on, Anyway?

An erupting Mount Vesuvius bombed a U.S. airstrip with hot ash and rocks during World War II, melting holes in more than fifty planes. Perhaps it was payback for a U.S. attack on a Hawaiian volcano in 1935. U.S. planes dropped twenty bombs in the path of a lava flow, turning it away from a city.

23D BOMB SQUADRON

Flying the Dusty Skies

Volcanic dust in the air is a big problem for airliners, even thousands of miles from a volcano. Floating dust looks like a regular cloud, but it can scrape the paint off planes and even clog their engines.

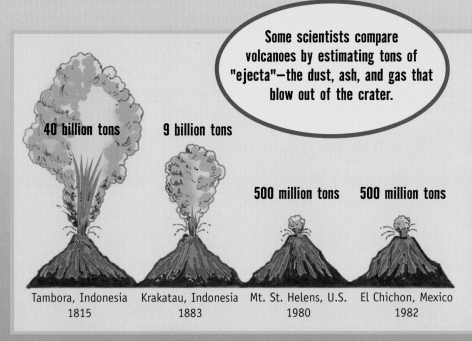

Some scientists compare volcanoes by estimating tons of "ejecta"—the dust, ash, and gas that blow out of the crater.

40 billion tons

9 billion tons

500 million tons

500 million tons

Tambora, Indonesia
1815

Krakatau, Indonesia
1883

Mt. St. Helens, U.S.
1980

El Chichon, Mexico
1982

How Do They Measure Up?

Maybe you've heard of the Richter scale for earthquakes or the F-scale for tornadoes. These measurements let scientists compare one earthquake or one tornado with another. But what about comparing volcanic eruptions? Is there one way to measure a volcano? Well, actually...not quite. Some scientists look at the height of the eruption column (how high material rises in the sky). Others look at the volume of material erupted (how much debris comes out). Still other scientists consider the distance stuff flies, how much gas comes out, and how long the eruption lasts. Unless you're comparing the same things, it makes it hard to compare one volcano with another.

100 Percent Chance of Ash

In Japan, the Sakurajima volcano erupts up to four hundred times per year, and residents listen for ashfall reports on the radio. Ash is shoveled like snow, and, instead of snowmen, kids make ashmen. Kids are also required to wear hard hats to school every day.

Ash from a cloud at the Sakurajima volcano covers the sidewalks like snow.

Olympus Mons, the largest volcano on Mars, covers an area the size of Texas!

Volcanoes in Space

The next time you want to see lava, just look at the Moon. Those large darkish areas are huge old lava fields. Volcanoes on the Moon, Mercury, and Mars have been dead for millions of years. These days, the most active volcanoes in our solar system are on Earth and on Io (EYE-oh)—one of Jupiter's moons.

Idaho Digs Volcanoes

You can thank ancient volcanic dust for today's world-famous Idaho potatoes. Spuds love to grow in that mineral-rich volcanic soil. Volcanic dust also helps grapes grow on the slopes of Mount Vesuvius and coffee beans thrive in the mountains of Colombia.

MAY I TAKE YOUR

ARE YOU INTO VOLCANOES? OF COURSE.

You're reading this book. But there are some people who are *really* into volcanoes— scientists called volcanologists (vul- cunn-ALL-uh-jists). Whether poking around in a crater that's been quiet for ten thousand years, dodging a brand-new lava flow, or sitting at a computer comparing worldwide eruption data, volcanologists teach us plenty about our planet.

Volcanologists study many things—the temperatures, movements, and contents of lava and gases. The movements of mountains. The history and timing of past eruptions. Sometimes they spend weeks camping on a volcano, just looking, listening, and taking notes and photographs. Then they might spend weeks thinking and writing about what

Phew! It stinks. It's hot. It's dangerous. And I love it!

they've seen, heard, and felt. Much of their work is aimed at an important goal—learning how to predict eruptions in order to save lives.

Volcanologists also help us understand how gases and dust affect the weather, how heat and pressure turn chemicals into minerals, and even how the Earth's inner furnace may someday provide humans with a clean, unlimited supply of energy.

TEMPERATURE?

It's Volcano Fever. Definitely.

The most daring volcanologists and volcano photographers of all time were probably Maurice and Katia Krafft of France. This husband-and-wife team met in college and were immediately drawn together by their love for volcanoes. For the next thirty years they traveled wherever volcanoes were erupting. They saw, wrote about, and photographed more eruptions than anyone else in the world, and they added much to our understanding of volcanoes. The Kraffts got some of their biggest thrills doing things no one else would do. Early films show them poking around in lava flows while acid gas eats holes in their pants. Later they wore fireproof suits and walked along the rim of an erupting crater. To measure the depth of an acid lake, they floated around in a flimsy rubber boat—until acid ate through the metal measuring cable.

Getting into an active volcano can mean wearing special protective gear that reflects heat—but makes it hard to see where you're going. One wrong step can send a volcanologist into a 2,000°F pool of lava. Instant incineration.

Maurice said other volcanologists thought he and Katia were crazy, but that was okay because "volcanoes are crazy." He said his dream was to slide down a lava flow in a fireproof canoe, taking measurements and photos along the way.

On June 3, 1991, the amazing career of Maurice and Katia came to an end while they were photographing pyroclastic flows in Japan. One flow took an unexpected turn, engulfed them, and killed them instantly. It was a sad day for volcanology.

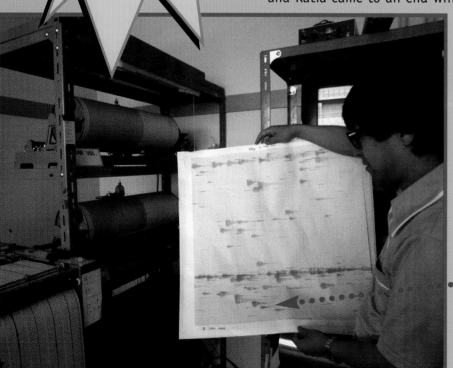

Volcanologists are often associated with a university, the United States Geological Survey (USGS), or a volcano observatory—a structure near or on a volcano specially designed for watching and taking measurements. There are observatories on or near about thirty-five volcanoes throughout the world.

A MORE PEACEFUL

NOT ALL CAREERS IN VOLCANOLOGY ARE AS WILD
as the Kraffts'. Dr. Richard V. Fisher, geology professor at the University of California at Santa Barbara, has a different approach. He's spent over forty years traveling the entire world, studying the effects of old eruptions.

Whether he's chipping away at a lava field in China or visiting the city devastated by Mount Pelée, R.V. (as he likes to be called) has a big love of nature and life that won't let him take dangerous chances.

His writings are full of volcano science, but they also contain beautiful, almost poetic descriptions of the locations he's visited. R.V.'s love of art, literature, and science began as a boy in California. He played piano, loved to read the travel adventures of Richard Halliburton, and collected rocks. Though he entered college as a music major, he graduated with a degree in geology. In his army years he witnessed an early test of an atomic bomb. He was later able to use what he saw to help explain volcanic pyroclastic flows. After all these years, R.V. still delights in the wonder of science. "To me, science is a kid following a bug and wondering what it is," he said.

Think About This:

Most volcano scientists have college degrees in geology. But the work really begins in high school. Future volcanologists should pay special attention to classes like biology, chemistry, physics, Earth science, algebra, trigonometry, and pre-calculus.

APPROACH

Future Fire

Most of our knowledge about volcanoes is new. Heck, the U.S. space program is older than the tectonic plate theory. We've learned a lot in a short time, and we're learning more every day.

Things are changing fast. Now special instruments in planes and satellites can help us "see" the Earth's hot spots, and the Internet helps us communicate the data instantly. Soon, a surprise volcano like Parícutin will probably be no surprise at all. And we won't have to wait for rumblings and earthquakes to know a volcano like Mount St. Helens is coming back to life.

Earth's hot spots as seen from a satellite camera.

Even simple things like better off-road vehicles are helping to expand our knowledge of volcanoes. Scientists can now reach out-of-the-way volcanoes without learning how to ride donkeys. Disasters often lead to scientific advancements, too. A volcanologist almost killed by flying rocks while studying a volcano decided to do something about it. He developed a way to take gas readings from a safe distance.

Exploring space will also help us understand our own volcanoes. What is it about Earth and Io that make them the two most volcanic bodies in our solar system?

Learning about volcanoes will never stop eruptions. They're just too powerful. But new understanding of pyroclastic flows, lahars, and the action of volcanic gases can help save lives. Since 1986, the USGS sends quick-response teams to check out the dangers of any volcano that's threatening to erupt.

Volcanologists and construction engineers are working together to invent ways to protect humans and property from volcanic debris. In Iceland they've already saved a town by spraying huge amounts of seawater on hot lava. And in Japan, debris channels built on some volcano sides divert rocks and lahars away from houses. It's only the beginning.

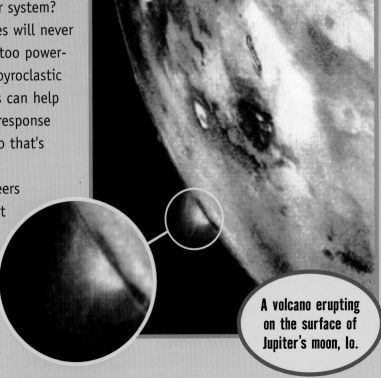

A volcano erupting on the surface of Jupiter's moon, Io.

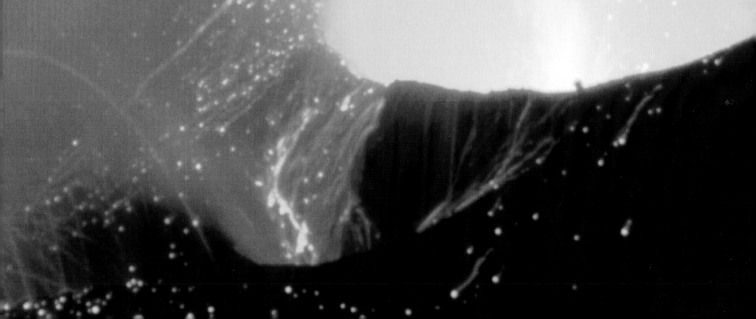

STAYING COOL AT

IF YOU'RE EVER DIGGING FOR WORMS TO GO FISHING, and lava starts flowing out of the hole, DO NOT continue digging. Notify the authorities immediately. Then find somewhere else to dig.

With only one brand-new volcano that we know about in all of human history, you probably don't have to worry about a worm barbeque opening up in your backyard. But the U.S. government does have some ideas for people who live near active volcanoes:

2,000°F

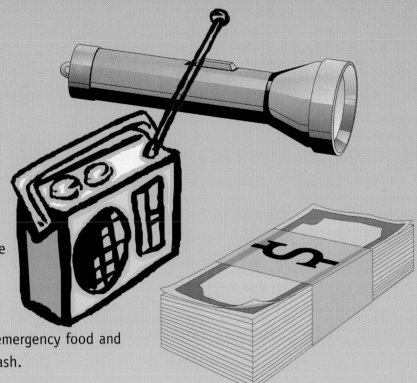

Have Disaster Supplies Ready

Have a pair of goggles and throwaway breathing masks for everyone in your household. In addition, have an all-purpose emergency kit ready to go—it can also be used in storms, power failures, etc. It should include a flashlight, portable radio, and extra batteries for both; first-aid kit; emergency food and water; nonelectric can opener; and extra cash.

Eruptions Don't Come Alone

Be prepared for earthquakes, flash floods, landslides, mudflows, dangerous lightning, and tsunamis. Avoid low-lying valleys and areas where poisonous gases can collect.

Ashfall Is Tricky

It may look like snow, but it's rock. Rooftop ashfalls can cause buildings to collapse. Breathing particles while clearing ashfalls can also be deadly. Driving vehicles through ash can quickly clog engines.

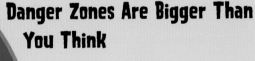

Danger Zones Are Bigger Than You Think

Hot rocks can easily fly twenty miles. Floods, heavy ash, and poisonous fumes can travel one hundred miles. Trying to experience an erupting volcano in person may be a very bad idea. As they said in Parícutin back in 1943, ¡Vamonos! (VA-mo-nose—Spanish for "Let's get OUTTA here!!")

The Volcano Glossary:
Explosive Definitions & Extra Info, Served Up Quick & Hot

avalanche the sudden movement of material down a mountainside. Most people think "snow" when they hear the word *avalanche,* but with a volcano it can be snow, ice, rock, mud, cinders, ash. Whatever is up there on that shaky slope is just waiting to come down.

ballistic projectile anything rocky that flies out of volcanoes, especially a rock that flies sideways. Rocks as big as cars can fly for miles.

caldera a low spot on the Earth where a volcano has erupted. Sometimes when magma comes out of a volcano, it leaves a huge empty magma chamber (like a cavern) underground. Then the weight of the volcano collapses the empty chamber. What's left on the surface is a low place called a caldera. Sometimes it fills with water and becomes a lake.

cinder cone a type of volcano in which lava fragments blow out of the Earth, harden into rock chips called cinders, and fall along with ash all around the volcano's crater. The cinders and ash pile up and can create a mountain shaped like a giant anthill.

composite (kom-PAW-zit) **volcano** also called a stratovolcano, this type of volcano is created by layer upon layer of cinders, ash, and hardened lava flows. It sometimes has lines of hardened lava along its sides. It's the classic type of volcano often shown in drawings and movies.

core the hot center of the Earth. At about 9,000°F, the iron and nickel there should be melted, but it's so tightly packed with atoms that it remains a solid ball, eight hundred miles across. Surrounding the solid inner core is a melted layer, about 1,400 miles thick, called the liquid outer core.

crust the cool outer layer of the Earth, which forms our continents and ocean bottoms. It is about thirty miles thick under the continents and three to five miles thick under the oceans.

Io (EYE-oh) one of Jupiter's sixteen moons. Considered the most active volcanic body in our solar system, the surface of Io is constantly changing because of eruptions.

kimberlite pipe a passage into the Earth at the site of an ancient volcano. Often the volcano is completely gone and the passage is filled with dirt and debris. Kimberlites can be the sites of many diamonds, produced millions of years earlier by the volcano's heat and pressure.

lahar (luh-HARR) huge amounts of water and debris rushing down a volcano's slope. It can happen when an eruption instantly melts ice and snow, when lakes on a volcano suddenly drain during an eruption, or even when heavy rain mixes with ash and debris. A lahar can rage for many miles, sweeping away everything in its path.

lava magma that stays melted for a while after it comes out of the Earth

lava dome a type of volcano, or part of a volcano, in which lava oozes out of the Earth, but is too thick to flow. Instead, the surface of the lava cools and hardens, but underneath, it's still hot and oozing. The crusty blob or "dome" sometimes grows until it explodes.

magma melted material inside a planet or moon

magnetism an attraction for metal found in some rocks formed by volcanoes. Scientists think magnetism results when heat bakes a rock's electrons into a certain pattern. Electrons are parts of the atoms that make up everything in the universe.

mantle the hot layers of melted material under the Earth's crust. It's about two thousand miles thick. Some layers are like melted tar; other layers are more solid.

pumice (PUM-miss) powder made from cooled, solid lava. It can be made naturally when small lava particles blow out of a volcano, or it can be made by crushing lava rocks. People sometimes use it as a scrubbing powder to clean things.

pyroclastic (PIE-row-class-stick) **flow** rocks, ash, gases, and lava from a volcano can fly thousands of feet into the air. Then it all comes down fast, hot, and unstoppable. This hot cloud, called a pyroclastic flow, can rush along the ground at two hundred miles per hour, burning everything in its path.

radioactivity one of the energy forces that creates heat and melting inside the Earth (or inside other planets or moons). It's caused by atoms in the Earth's core changing their form and giving off heat and light.

shield volcano a type of volcano in which thin, runny lava flows in many directions, hardens, and slowly builds a wide, flat-topped mountain. Over millions of years, the mountain can become very wide and very high.

subduction (sub-DUCK-shun) the edge of one tectonic plate slowly working its way under the edge of another tectonic plate. The edge that moves down into the hot mantle can melt and become magma.

submarine *sub* means "below." *Marine* means "related to the sea." So, these types of volcanoes are "below the sea." They're the most common type of volcano because most of the Earth's crust is below the sea. Sometimes the material that comes out piles up high enough to rise above the sea and become an island.

tectonic plate also called a crustal plate. The Earth's crust is cracked into about a dozen or more interlocking pieces that float on the hot mantle. The pieces are huge, holding continents and oceans. Each piece is called a tectonic plate, which means "structural" plate.

tephra fall like snowfall, if snow were made of rock. It can be cinders, ash, or a fine powder called pumice. Because it's basically rock, it's very heavy. It can pile up on a rooftop and crush a house.

tsunami (soo-NOM-mee) a wall of water that can travel hundreds of miles per hour. Tsunamis are usually caused when seawater is shoved by an earthquake, but they can also be caused by a pyroclastic flow hitting water. Sometimes tsunamis are wrongly called tidal waves.

United States Geological Survey also known as USGS, it's considered one of the world's leading earth sciences organizations. Its scientists study and map earthquakes and floods as well as volcanoes. Whenever a volcano threatens to erupt, a USGS quick-response team rushes to the scene to investigate the volcano and help save lives.

volcanic gas the gas that comes out of a volcano's superheated and melted rocks. Sometimes it's people-friendly gas like oxygen; sometimes it's deadly like carbon monoxide.

volcano a vent, hole, or weak spot in the crust of a planet or moon where hot materials and gases can escape from inside

volcano observatory a structure on or near a volcano where volcanologists can watch and take measurements. There are observatories at about thirty-five volcanoes worldwide.

volcanologist (vul-cunn-ALL-uh-jist) a scientist who studies volcanoes

volcanology the study of volcanoes

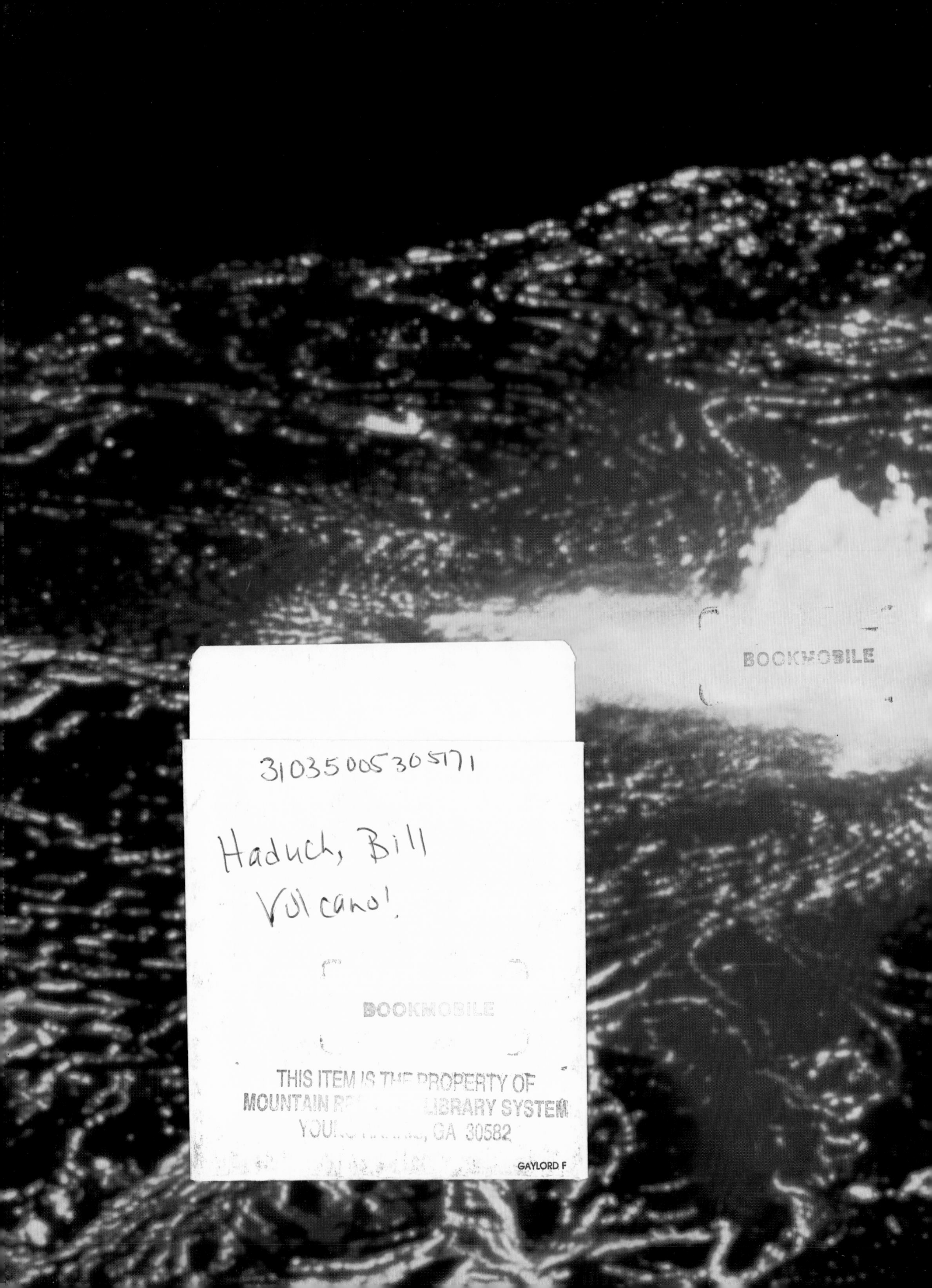